ANGER MANAGEMENT FOR PARENTS

PARENTING WITH COMPASSION AND UNDERSTANDING

BARBARA G. COLLINS

Table of contents

Introduction

Sharon had been married for 10 years and had three children. She was always a happy and loving mother, but lately something had changed. She was feeling increasingly angry and helpless, unable to control her emotions.

One day, after an intense argument with her husband, Sharon decided to take a walk in the park. She sat down on a bench and stared at the pond, her mind in a jumble.

Suddenly, she noticed a book lying on the bench. It was titled "Anger Management for Parents." authored by Barbara G. Collins picked it up and started reading.

The book talked about the causes of anger and how to identify triggers and react appropriately. It suggested techniques such as deep breathing and visualization to reduce stress and gain control of one's emotions.

Sharon started applying the techniques she learnt from this book. Whenever she felt herself getting angry, she would take a few deep breaths and visualize a peaceful scene, like a beach or a mountain. She also began to look at situations from different points of view, which helped her to better understand and accept them.

Slowly but surely, Sharon felt her anger dissipating. She was now able to better manage her emotions and was no longer feeling helpless.

Sharon was a changed person. She was calmer, more patient and understanding. She was also able to communicate better with her husband and her children.

Sharon had learnt a valuable lesson from this book that anger is a natural emotion and it can be managed with the right techniques. She was glad that she had taken the time to read this book on anger management and was now able to live a peaceful and fulfilling life.

It was a journey that began with a single book, and Sharon was thankful for it.

Anger is an emotion that we all experience. It is a normal response to feeling threatened, frustrated, or powerless. It is how we express our displeasure with something or someone, and it can be a healthy way to express our feelings. However, when anger becomes uncontrolled, it can have serious consequences for both the person experiencing it and for those around them. Parents must be aware of the signs that their child is struggling with anger and be prepared to take proactive steps in order to manage it.

It is important to remember that anger management is not just about controlling a child's behavior, but rather helping them understand the causes of their anger and teaching them better ways to express it. As such, it is important to start by addressing the root causes of anger in a child, such as lack of self-esteem, poor communication skills, or an unmet need.

Once these underlying issues have been addressed, parents can then work with their children to develop effective coping skills and strategies for managing their anger.

This may include teaching children about the physical and emotional signs of anger, helping them practice relaxation techniques, and helping them learn to identify triggers and respond appropriately. Additionally, parents should provide a safe and supportive environment for their children to express their

frustrations and anger, while also setting clear limits and boundaries. By providing an understanding and supportive environment while also teaching children appropriate ways to express their anger, parents can help them learn to manage their anger in a healthy way.

Anger management for parents is an important step in helping children develop emotional intelligence and self-control. It is important for parents to be patient and understanding of their children's feelings and reactions and to provide support and guidance in helping them learn to manage their anger. With the right approach, parents can help their children learn to manage their anger in a healthy way that will benefit them in the long-term.

Chapter 1

Understanding Anger

1. Define Anger: Before attempting to understand anger, it is essential to gain a clear understanding of what it is. Anger is an emotion, usually involving strong feelings of frustration, irritation, or annoyance, often triggered by a perceived wrong or injustice. It is a normal, healthy emotion, but it can become problematic if it is not managed properly.

2. Identify the Sources of Anger: Once you have a clear understanding of anger, the next step is to identify the sources of anger. Common sources of anger include feelings of helplessness, injustice, hurt, or frustration. It is important to be aware of the triggers of your own anger, so that you can take steps to manage it more effectively.

3. Understand the Physiological Impact of Anger: It is also important to understand the physiological impact of anger. Anger can cause physical changes in the body, such as increased heart rate and blood pressure, muscle tension, and a heightened state of alertness. It is important to be aware of these physical changes, and to recognize when they occur.

4. Develop Healthy Coping Strategies: Developing healthy coping strategies can help to manage anger. This can include distraction techniques, relaxation exercises, and positive self-talk.

5.Identify Unhelpful Thinking Patterns: Unhelpful thinking patterns can increase feelings of anger, so it is important to identify them and work to change them. This could involve challenging irrational beliefs, or recognizing and reframing negative thoughts.

6. Seek Professional Help: If you are struggling to manage your anger, it is important to seek professional help. A qualified mental health professional can help you to develop effective strategies for managing your anger.

These are just a few ways that could assist you to understand anger. With the right approach, a powerful book on understanding anger can help readers to gain insight into their own anger, and to develop healthy strategies for managing it.

Chapter 2

Causes of Anger

Anger is a natural emotion that can be triggered by a variety of situations. It is a response to perceived provocation, hurt, or injustice. People can experience anger in response to both real and imagined slights.

Causes of anger can include frustration, disappointment, injustice, feeling unheard or disregarded, and even physical pain. Some people are more prone to anger than others due to their genetic makeup and personality traits. In addition, people can learn to express anger in unhealthy ways, leading to a tendency to become angry more easily.

Common causes of anger include:

1. Frustration: This occurs when expectations aren't met, goals aren't reached, or progress is blocked.

2. Disappointment: This can occur when a person feels let down by someone or something.

3. Injustice: This can occur when a person feels they have been treated unfairly or wronged in some way.

4. Feeling unheard or disregarded: This can occur when a person feels their feelings or opinions have been ignored or disregarded.

5. Physical pain: This can occur when a person is in physical pain and is unable to find relief.

6. Stress: This can occur when a person is overwhelmed or overburdened by their responsibilities or obligations.

7. Conflict: This can occur when a person feels they are in disagreement with someone or something.

8. Fear: This can occur when a person feels threatened or uncertain.

9. Jealousy: This can occur when a person feels threatened by or envious of someone else.

10. Shame or humiliation: This can occur when a person feels embarrassed or ashamed.

It is important to understand the causes of anger so that we can better manage our emotions. Taking steps to understand why we get angry and finding healthier ways to cope with our anger can help us lead happier and healthier lives.

In addition to the above causes, anger can also be triggered by chemical imbalances in the brain, such as those caused by depression or anxiety. These imbalances can cause a person to become more irritable and prone to outbursts of anger. It is important to seek treatment if you are struggling with mental health issues that may be triggering or worsening your anger.

Anger can happen when a person feels powerless or out of control. In these cases, it is important to find ways to regain control and to practice self-care. Taking deep breaths, engaging in relaxation techniques, or talking to a trusted friend can help to reduce feelings of anger.

It is important to remember that anger is a normal emotion and that it is not always bad. It can be used to motivate positive change or to bring attention to an important issue. However, it is important to remember that anger can be destructive if it is not managed properly.

Taking steps to understand the cause of your anger and to find healthier ways to cope can help you manage your anger in a healthy way.

1. Unmet Expectations: As parents, we have expectations of our children and ourselves as parents. When these expectations are not met, it can lead to feelings of frustration, disappointment, and anger.

2. Lack of Respect: When children don't show respect for their parents, it can be a real source of anger. Respect is something that needs to be earned and taught, but when it's lacking it can make parents feel powerless and angry.

3. Disobedience: Children not following instructions or disobeying can cause parents to feel angry and frustrated. Parents often feel like they're not being taken seriously and that their words don't have any weight.

4. Inappropriate Behavior: If a child is engaging in inappropriate behavior, it can be a source of anger for parents. This could include things like swearing, making fun of others, or engaging in risky behavior.

5. Stress: Parenting can be a stressful job. When parents are struggling with their own stress levels, it can be difficult for them to keep their emotions in check. This can lead to outbursts of anger when things don't go as planned.

6. Unreasonable Demands: When parents feel like their children are making unreasonable demands, it can be a source of anger. This could include things like constantly asking for money or wanting more than their parents are able to give.

7. Difference of Opinion: When parents and children have different opinions or beliefs, it can cause a lot of tension and disagreement. This can lead to feelings of anger from both sides.

8. Fear of Failure: Parents may feel angry if they feel like their children are not reaching their potential. This could be because of a fear of failure or not living up to their expectations.

Chapter 3

Warning Signs of Anger

1. Body Language: Body language is a good indicator of anger. Someone who is angry may have a tense posture, clenched fists, and they may be glaring or scowling. They may also be fidgeting or pacing.

2. Verbal Cues: Someone who is angry may raise their voice, use harsh language, or talk in an aggressive manner. They may also be easily agitated or argumentative.

3. Physical Symptoms: Physical symptoms of anger can include tightness in the chest, increased heart rate, flushing of the face, or increased sweating.

4. Thoughts: Thoughts related to anger may involve rumination, thoughts of revenge, or violent fantasies.

5. Emotions: Anger is a strong emotion that can take over and cause a person to act in ways they normally wouldn't. It can also be accompanied by other emotions such as frustration, irritability, or resentment.

6. Behaviors: Behaviors related to anger can include uncontrolled outbursts of rage, lashing out at others, or physical violence. It is important to be aware of the warning signs of anger so that you can intervene or de-escalate the situation before it gets out of hand.

If someone is exhibiting signs of anger, it is important to listen to them and remain calm. It can be helpful to try to understand the other person's perspective and to give them space to express their feelings. It is also important to keep yourself safe if the situation becomes too intense.

• **Increased Verbal Aggression:** Watch out for verbal aggression, such as yelling, cursing, or saying things that are intended to hurt or humiliate.

• **Physically Aggressive Behavior:** Physically aggressive behavior can manifest as hitting, kicking, or throwing objects.

• **Withdrawal:** A child may withdraw from activities or people they once enjoyed.

- **Aggressive Play:** If your child is engaging in aggressive play with toys and other children, this can be a sign of anger.

- **Destructive Behavior:** Destructive behavior, such as tearing up books or breaking objects, can be a sign of anger.

- **Irritability:** If your child is easily irritable and has frequent outbursts, this could be a sign of anger.

- **Unreasonable Expectations:** If your child is making unreasonable demands or expectations, this could be a sign of anger.

- **Uncooperative Attitude:** If your child is refusing to cooperate or take direction, this could be a sign of anger.

relaxation techniques, parents can effectively manage their anger and foster a respectful and loving relationship with their children.

www.ingramcontent.com/pod-product-compliance
Lightning Source LLC
LaVergne TN
LVHW050330160826
845677LV00014B/3585

* 9 7 9 8 3 7 3 1 7 8 1 4 3 *